A PICTURE BOOK OF
Cesar Chavez

by David A. Adler and Michael S. Adler

illustrated by Marie Olofsdotter

Holiday House / New York

For my son, Yoni
M. S. A.

For my grandson, Yoni
D. A. A.

For our Tierra Madre, Mother Earth
M. O.

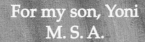

Text copyright © 2010 by David A. Adler and Michael S. Adler
Illustrations copyright © 2010 by Marie Olofsdotter
All Rights Reserved
HOLIDAY HOUSE is registered in the
U.S. Patent and Trademark Office.
Printed and Bound in April 2010 at Kwong Fat Offset Printing Co., Ltd., Dongguan City,
Quangdong Province, China.
www.holidayhouse.com
First Edition
1 3 5 7 9 10 8 6 4 2

Library of Congress Cataloging-in-Publication Data
Adler, David A.
A picture book of Cesar Chavez / by David A. Adler and Michael S. Adler ;
illustrated by Marie Olofsdotter. — 1st ed.
p. cm.
ISBN 978-0-8234-2202-9 (hardcover)
1. Chavez, Cesar, 1927-1993—Juvenile literature. 2. United Farm Workers—History—Juvenile literature.
3. Labor leaders—United States—Biography—Juvenile literature. 4. Mexican American migrant
agricultural laborers—Biography—Juvenile literature. 5. Migrant agricultural laborers—Labor unions—
United States—History—Juvenile literature. I. Adler, Michael S. II. Olofsdotter, Marie, 1957- III. Title.
HD6509.C48A35 2010
331.88'13092—dc22
[B]
2009039319

As a child, Cesar Chavez traveled with his family from one farm to the next to pick beans, broccoli, lettuce, and other crops. After a day in the fields, his back often ached. His hands were sore. Yet Chavez and others who helped put food on Americans' tables often had no tables of their own, no real homes. Later, Cesar Chavez would lead the fight for better pay, working conditions, and health care for families such as his.

Cesar Chavez was born on March 31, 1927, near Yuma, Arizona. His parents, Librado and Juana Chavez, were farmers. Cesar was the second of their five children.

Cesar's father was often too busy to spend time with his family. It was Cesar's mom who kept them together. She told her children stories. She taught them values and many proverbs, such as "What you do to others, others do to you."

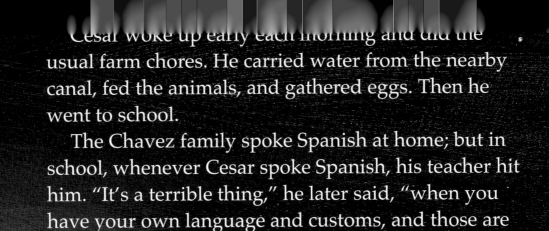

Cesar woke up early each morning and did the usual farm chores. He carried water from the nearby canal, fed the animals, and gathered eggs. Then he went to school.

The Chavez family spoke Spanish at home; but in school, whenever Cesar spoke Spanish, his teacher hit him. "It's a terrible thing," he later said, "when you have your own language and customs, and those are shattered."

Cesar Chavez grew up during the Great Depression. People everywhere lost their jobs. In 1938, Cesar's parents lost their farm and moved to California.

Cesar's father soon found work for the family picking peas. They walked, bent over, between the rows of plants. For a full hamper—twenty-five pounds of peas—they earned twenty cents. When the work on that farm was done, the family moved on.

They picked string beans, lima beans, broccoli, lettuce, sugar beets, cauliflower, onions, carrots, tomatoes, cantaloupe, watermelon, and grapes. When the farm boss was especially unfair or when work conditions were especially bad, Cesar's father said, "Okay, let's go," and they quit. Cesar Chavez later remembered, "Our dignity meant more than money."

The Chavez family, like many others, had no real home. One winter, with nowhere else to go, they slept in a tent in a woman's yard.

The family moved around so much that Cesar attended sixty-five elementary schools, some for just a day or a week. In 1942, after his father was hurt in a car accident, fifteen-year-old Cesar dropped out of school to earn money for his family.

In 1944, in the midst of World War II, Cesar Chavez enlisted in the U.S. Navy. He served for two years. While on a short leave, he went to a movie theater in Delano, California. The theater was segregated. African Americans, Filipinos, and Mexicans were confined to a section on the right. Cesar Chavez felt this was wrong. He sat on the left and was arrested.

"In our own way," Chavez said later, "my family had been challenging the growers for some time." Now he was challenging a theater owner.

After his discharge from the navy, Chavez began dating Helen Fabela, a young woman from a family of farmworkers. Helen worked in a local grocery store, and Chavez went to the store often just to see her. They married in 1948 and soon moved to San Jose, California. They had eight children.

In June 1952, Chavez met Fred Ross, who had been sent to San Jose by the Community Service Organization (CSO) to register voters for the coming elections. "He changed my life," Chavez said.

Ross explained how in the United States even poor people had power. They just needed to speak out, to vote. Chavez was convinced and went door-to-door and urged people to register to vote.

At first he was so frightened he couldn't talk. "Little by little I got confidence," Chavez said later. "In about three days I was doing okay."

Chavez talked and argued with people and would not give up until they agreed to register. Soon he was hired to start CSO chapters throughout California.

In 1958, he went to Oxnard and asked the farmworkers there to register and vote. They asked him, "Why is it we can't get any jobs?" The jobs were going to workers from Mexico, who accepted lower pay.

Chavez organized a march. Reporters came and saw Chavez stand on the hood of a car and speak to the out-of-work farmworkers. After a thirteen-month struggle, the Oxnard fruit growers gave in and hired local workers.

In 1962, Chavez left the CSO and formed a fruit pickers union, the National Farm Workers Association (NFWA). By 1965 it had seventeen hundred member families. California grape pickers were paid about one dollar an hour, which was not a living wage. From that dollar, some growers charged the workers, who spent all day in the hot sun, for every drink of water they took. In September 1965, workers in another union began a strike against grape growers in Delano. Chavez's union joined them. The two unions merged, forming the United Farm Workers Organizing Committee (UFWOC).

Chavez organized church meetings, sit-ins, and even
a three-hundred-mile march of underpaid California
grape pickers. When all that failed, he called for a
nationwide boycott of California grapes. In February
1968, in protest, Chavez stopped eating. For twenty-
five days straight he drank only water and diet soda.
His followers rallied behind him.

Cesar's fast ended at a public mass and celebration. "I was so much out of it," Chavez said later. "All I felt was a lot of people pushing and trying to get closer. . . . I was being held up because my legs were so weak."

Senator Robert F. Kennedy gave Chavez a piece of bread to eat. "I come here as an American citizen to honor Cesar Chavez," Kennedy said. "I honor him for his compassion, his honesty, his truth, and dedication."

The strike and boycott ended in July 1970 with higher wages and health care protection for members of Chavez's union.

Chavez wasn't done fighting for poor farmworkers.

In August 1970, he called for a boycott of lettuce; and when he refused to end the boycott despite a court order, he was thrown in jail. In 1972, he fasted for twenty-four days to protest antiunion laws. He organized a massive voter registration drive that helped defeat those laws.

Chavez knew that poisonous chemicals sprayed on grapevines to keep away insects were injuring farmworkers. In 1987, he called for a boycott of all grapes sprayed with dangerous pesticides and fasted for thirty-six days in support of the boycott. In the years ahead, laws were passed to limit the use of these chemicals.

In April 1993, Chavez died in his sleep while on union business in Arizona. American farmworkers had lost their greatest champion. In accordance with his wishes, he was buried in a simple pine box. More than forty thousand people marched in his procession.

One year later, Helen Chavez accepted the Presidential Medal of Freedom, the nation's highest civilian honor, for her husband. At the ceremony, President Bill Clinton said, "This remarkable man . . . with faith and discipline, with soft-spoken humility and amazing inner strength, led a very courageous life. And in so doing, he brought dignity to the lives of so many others and provided for us inspiration for the rest of our nation's history."

IMPORTANT DATES

1927 Born near Yuma, Arizona, March 31.

1938 Moves with his family to California.

1942 Quits school to work full-time and help support his family.

1944 Enlists in the United States Navy.

1948 Marries Helen Fabela, a fellow migrant worker from Delano, Cesar's hometown.

1952 Meets Fred Ross. Begins work with the Community Service Organization (CSO), June.

1962 Forms the National Farm Workers Association (NFWA).

1965 Joins a strike against grape growers. Leads a boycott of grapes in an appeal for fair wages.

1968 Twenty-five-day fast to ensure his grape protest remains nonviolent.

1970 Reaches agreement for higher wages and better working conditions for farmworkers with twenty-three California grape growers.

1972 Twenty-four-day fast to protest antiunion laws passed by Arizona governor Jack Williams.

1974 California passes the Agricultural Labor Relations Act, the first bill of rights for farmworkers passed in the United States.

1987 Calls for a boycott of all grapes sprayed with dangerous pesticides.

1988 Thirty-six-day fast in support of the grape boycott.

1993 Dies in San Luis, Arizona, April 23.

1994 Awarded the Presidential Medal of Freedom, the nation's highest civilian honor.

SOURCE NOTES

Each source note includes the first word or words and the last word or words of a quotation and its source. References are to books cited in the Selected Bibliography.

"It's a . . . are shattered.": Levy, p. 24.

"Okay, let's go . . . than money.": Ibid., pp. 78–79.

"In our own . . . for some time.": Ibid., p. 85.

"He changed my life.": Ibid., p. 93.

"Little by . . . was doing okay.": Ibid., p. 104.

"Why is . . . any jobs?": Ibid., p. 129.

"I was . . . so weak.": Ibid., p. 286.

"I come here . . . and dedication.": Day, p. 48.

"This remarkable . . . nation's history.": Ferriss, back cover.

Ferriss, Susan, and Richard Sandoval. *The Fight in the Fields: Cesar Chavez and the Farmworkers Movement.* New York: Harcourt Brace & Company, 1997.

Levy, Jacques. *Cesar Chavez, Autobiography of La Causa.* New York: W. W. Norton, 1975.

Lindsey, Robert. "Cesar Chavez, 66, Organizer of Union For Migrants, Dies." *New York Times*, April 24, 1993, pp. 1, 29.

Matthiessen, Peter. *Sal Si Puedes (Escape If You Can): Cesar Chavez and the New American Revolution.* Berkeley: University of California Press, 1969.

Rodriguez, Consuelo. *Cesar Chavez.* New York: Chelsea House Publishers, 1991.

SELECTED BIBLIOGRAPHY

Day, Mark. *Forty Acres: Cesar Chavez and the Farm Workers.* New York: Praeger Publishers, 1971.

RECOMMENDED WEBSITES

www.ufw.org

www.cesarechavezfoundation.org

www.epcc.edu/ftp/Homes/monicaw/borderlands/15_cesar_chavez.htm

AUTHORS' NOTES

There is a difference of opinion concerning the number of children Librado and Juana had. Many sources say five, others say six. At Cesar Chavez's death the *New York Times* reported he was the second of five children, but also that he was survived by three brothers and two sisters.

Fred Ross's responsibilities included organizing Latino communities. Fred's son later commented that his father "had a lot of anger about injustice, and he couldn't live with himself if he wasn't doing something about it." Ross maintained a friendship with Cesar Chavez and helped Cesar plan the 1965 strike against the San Joaquin Valley grape growers.

Hunger strikes are sometimes used as a peaceful way to call attention to a cause. Before Chavez, Mohandas Gandhi (1869–1948) of India had fasted several times to end prejudice and bring attention to his nation's struggle for freedom.

The UFWOC became a member of the American Federation of Labor and Congress of Industrial Organizations (AFL-CIO) in 1971 and shortened its name to the United Farm Workers of America (UFW).